DARKROOM FAITH WORKOUTS

FAITH DEVELOPED IN THE DARKROOM SERIES

DARKROOM FAITH WORKOUTS

30 DAY DEVOTIONAL

DARRYL O. GRIFFIN, D. Div.

Darkroom Faith Workouts
30 Day Devotional

Published by Dr. Darryl O. Griffin
P.O. Box 1333
Cordova, TN 38088
www.darrylogriffin.com

ISBN: 978-1-7346581-2-5 Paperback
978-1-7346581-3-2 Digital

Printed in the United States of America

Contents

DAY
1
15 KG
FAITH
WORKOUT

DAY 1

FAITH WORKOUT

A moderate dose of fear may be considered normal, even healthy. It may be simply an awareness of impending danger—a defense mechanism. It may just be the heart rate increasing, voice elevation, and sweaty palms in anticipation of being called on in class or being asked to make a public speech at the company meeting. Fear may be a reaction to imagined or real circumstances. They can be acute or chronic. Many fearful people tend to infect others with their anxieties and tensions.

When dealing with a person infected with fear, you must demonstrate faith by walking in love and try to discover the root cause of the fear. You have probably heard that **"faith works through love."** This expression is found in Galatians 5:6. There may be no easy or instantaneous solutions to the problem; but you can suggest a proper relationship with Jesus Christ, dependence on the Holy Spirit, and a life focused on the Word of God daily as necessary steps to deliverance from the bondage of fear.

He Himself has said, "I will never leave you nor forsake you." ***So that we may boldly say, "The Lord is my helper, and I will not fear..." (Hebrews 13:5-6)***

There are many more Faith promises from God's Word that you can hold on to for peace and strength in the midst of your darkroom experiences. But perhaps the most precious faith-filled promise can be found in the powerful Words of Jesus: ***"I am with you always, even to the end of the world." (Matthew 28:20)*** And that is a very comforting spiritual truth.

What does today's Faith Workout Devotion teach you about overcoming your fears?

Spend some time in prayer addressing your fears.

WORKOUT REFLECTIONS

DAY
2
15 KG
FAITH
WORKOUT

DAY 2

FAITH WORKOUT

What we need while in the dark seasons of our lives is hope. Hope is an earnest expectation. It is the confident affirmation that God is faithful, that He will complete what He has begun. It is also, that confident expectation which waits patiently for God's purposes to be fulfilled. If we don't have hope, then we don't need faith. Hebrews 11:1 state, ***"Now faith is the substance of things hoped for, the evidence of things not seen."***

If you don't have hope, a goal, a vision, or a desire fueled by passion, then the message of hope I'm sharing with you will be meaningless. These are just words that mean nothing because the next incident that occurs in your life will wash these words away from your mind. If you are a person of purpose, focus, and tenacity and have hope that you can't reach or touch, then faith becomes the bridge between where you are and where you're trying to go. It is the substance of things hoped for and the evidence of things not seen. And yet, you can have the things that happened in life that knocked you over, knocked you down, or knocked the wind out of you that can handicap you. And suddenly, you feel incapacitated to perform in life as it relates to faith. ***Here are some Reasons You Should Have Hope Today:***

Hope because God hears you.

"Out of the depths I cry to you, O Lord! O Lord, hear my voice! Let your ears be attentive to the voice of my pleas for mercy!" (Psalm 130:1-2 ESV) These verses give us hope in our darkroom experiences because God hears us when we call, and we are never alone.

Hope because God speaks to you.

"I wait for the Lord, my soul waits, and in his word I hope." (Psalm 130:5 ESV)

Wow! What a revelation. God's living and active word is a miracle! You do not need to wait to hear from Him during dark seasons because all you need is to open your Bible. God's Word is the sword of the Spirit. Hope, because God gives you all you need to live victoriously; to be strengthened and to be equipped right here and right now.

What does today's Faith Workout Devotion teach you about your hope in God?

WORKOUT REFLECTIONS

DAY
3
15 KG
FAITH
WORKOUT

DAY 3
FAITH WORKOUT

Jesus said in John 10:10 that he came that we the believer might have life and having more abundantly.

While in the darkroom if I'm honest you may experience anxiety from time-to-time. Anxiety is simply the fear or phobia of danger and misfortune. Another source says it is the state of apprehension. Anxiety is a result of not being able to physically see while in the darkroom. Now, be prepared because you will experience anxiety in the darkroom that has at least three main elements. First, **Insecurity**—Sometimes you conjure up things in your mind that might happen because things look too good to be true. Secondly, **Helplessness**—this is the idea that you can't fix it.

Thirdly, **Isolation**—Remember God won't permit you to take anyone with you in the Darkroom. This is the idea of thinking, "Who is going to help me while I'm in here?" Isolation is the playground of the devil. The devil wants you in isolation so that he can interrogate you. As soon as the door is shut and the lights are turned off in the darkroom, you start experiencing anxiety, nervousness, you might feel out of control. Out of control is that disconnect between the body and your spirit. You start experiencing panic attacks, a lack of sleep, or lots of stress. This will make you lose the ability to trust God.

Anxiety will rob you of the ability to enjoy your life abundantly. You become so obsessed with what is going on, on the outside of the door of the Darkroom and you let it overwhelm you. The enemy's plan is to get you frustrated, so you will abort the plan of God for your life.

So, what do you do while experiencing Darkroom anxiety? Admit There is a Problem! We must admit that we have a problem. We are stressed and concerned about things we can't see in the Darkroom. Listen child of God, this doesn't mean that we are not spiritual, it simply means that we are transparent and honest with God. If you don't face it, you can't fix it.

"Blessed is the man to whom the Lord does not impute iniquity, And in whose spirit there is no deceit." (Psalm 32:2 NKJV)

While in the Darkroom, tell God the truth.

What does today's Faith Workout Devotion teach you about dealing with stress?

What are you stressed about today? Please make a list!

WORKOUT REFLECTIONS

DAY
4
15 KG
FAITH
WORKOUT

DAY 4
FAITH WORKOUT

Be intentional about what enters your mind—There are at least three gates to the life of a believer.

It starts with what you see or your sight, enforced by what you hear, then you start confessing, speaking about it from your mouth. We should take precautions for what we see, hear, and speak.

Philippians 4:8 NKJV – "Finally, brethren, whatever things are true, whatever things are noble, whatever things are just, whatever things are pure, whatever things are lovely, whatever things are of good report, if there is any virtue and if there is anything praiseworthy—meditate on these things."

It is critical in this season to know that everything you hear is not always true. You must learn while in the Darkroom to tune out all outside noises. The devil will whisper lies in your ear while you are going through moments of darkness. Meditation on the Word of God is not just emptying the mind of wrong or negative things, but also filling your mind with things that are righteous and of good report. But you must embrace the process—You must trust God to bring you through. You must make a decision today to trust and depend totally on God while in the Darkroom.

In Mark's gospel chapter 4, Jesus tells the disciples, let us pass over to the other side. Jesus gets into the ship, gets a pillow, and goes to sleep. A pop-up storm comes, and the disciples get nervous. They panic and awake Jesus. The disciples in verse 38 says, "Master," (meaning teacher) and ask, "Do you care if we die?" Jesus then asks, "Why are you so fearful? How is it that you have no faith?" Note that Jesus saying "Peace be still" is not the moral of the story as most may think. The moral of this story is when Jesus says, "Let us go over to the other side." In other words, if He uses the words "Let us go," then it is an indication that "us" is going to make it to the other side. If God told you that you are going to make it, stop panicking today! While in the Darkroom, it is impossible to be stressed out and trust God at the same time. It is time to trade in your panic for prayer, your fear for faith, your worry for God's peace, your weakness for His strength.

What does today's Faith Workout Devotion teach you about the three gates of the Believer?

WORKOUT REFLECTIONS

DAY
5
15 KG
FAITH
WORKOUT

DAY 5

FAITH WORKOUT

In the gospel according to Matthew chapter 7 vs 7, Jesus said: **"Ask, and it shall be given you; seek, and ye shall find; knock, and it shall be opened unto you:" (KJV)**

Question: How many times in the New Testament does the Bible say, "Ask and it shall be given?" The answer is 29. In Greek, this literally means, "Just keep on asking, to be consistent, to be continual." While in the Darkroom, you must **Anticipate It.** When you anticipate it, you prophesy, you expect, you foresee beforehand, you say that this thing will happen in my future, despite how dark it looks. I anticipate being healed, I anticipate my marriage being restored, I anticipate my business growing, I anticipate my children and grandchildren saved, I anticipate bigger, better, God's best for my life. But you must expect an answer in faith. Many Christians quit asking and seeking when they find themselves in the darkroom. May I encourage you today, if you want something first, you have to ask the right question. You have to ask the right way and that is asking, believing and not doubting. For example, when you ask for wisdom, the key is prayer, and the condition is faith.

"But without faith it is impossible to please Him, for he who comes to God must believe that He is, and that He is a rewarder of those who diligently seek Him." (Hebrews 11:6 NKJV)

While in our darkest moments, I believe He rewards us according to our faith. The verse says, "He rewards those who earnestly seek Him." It does not say who casually seek Him. It does not say who conveniently seek Him. It does not say who seeks Him once or twice a week, or when you feel like it. Now, to be fair, the word "earnestly" is not in the Greek. However, the word for seek is not an ordinary word for seek either. It actually implies to look with passion, or to be continually be absorbed in something or someone. I believe this should make all of us re-examine how we are seeking Him in moments of darkness. No one knows this better than you besides God Himself. So how much passion drives you to seeking the Father? How hard do you pursue after His Word? He rewards those who not just seek Him but seek Him with a burning zeal.

What does today's Faith Workout Devotion teach you about asking while in the Darkroom?

WORKOUT REFLECTIONS

DAY
6
15 KG
FAITH
WORKOUT

DAY 6

FAITH WORKOUT

While taking my photography class at the Art Institute of Atlanta, students not only took the pictures but developed them right there at the school campus in our darkroom. The film would be transferred somehow to some special paper and then the paper would be dipped in several different trays holding chemical solutions. As the photos were moved from tray to tray, the image which was always there began to emerge. This process took a substantial amount of time and care and seemed almost breathtaking.

Understandably, our teacher and those photographers would be highly upset if another student opened the darkroom door while going through this process. Too much light would rush in and expose every piece of negative on which they had been painfully laboring. It is not always the right thing to try to open the door for someone whose time of development is not up in the darkroom. This indeed is what I call, wasted development. The darkness of that darkroom made the proper development of those negatives possible so that everything else necessary to produce a memorable image could happen.

"For our light and momentary troubles are achieving for us an eternal glory that far outweighs them all. So we fix our eyes not on what is seen, but on what is unseen, since what is seen is temporary, but what is unseen is eternal." (2 Corinthians 4:17-18 NIV)

God allows darkroom experiences to develop our faith. When we are experiencing moments of darkness, financial hardship, failure, sickness, job loss, disappointment, divorce or one life blow after another; we need to look at things through "red" the blood of Jesus. Like the photographers, wait patiently inside the darkroom and watch as God takes His time and care to develop the picture of your life that He has taken. Today, don't rush through any of the stages; endure every "chemical bath." Only when the process is complete will you be fully developed. You will only be ready for the Master's use when His image emerges through you.

What does today's Faith Workout Devotion teach you about the development of negatives?

WORKOUT REFLECTIONS

DAY
7
15 KG
FAITH
WORKOUT

DAY 7

FAITH WORKOUT

While in the Darkroom, I have learned over the years that if you wait it out, God will work it out.

Job 14:13-14 KJV says, "O that thou wouldest hide me in the grave, that thou wouldest keep me secret, until thy wrath be past, that thou wouldest appoint me a set time, and remember me! If a man die, shall he live again? all the days of my appointed time will I wait, till my change come."

If there is anything that we learned about Job's situation, it is the fact that God is always working in the lives of His people. Even today, God is actively involved in the affairs of our lives. No matter how difficult the circumstances may be, you have to see the Hand of God in it.

What Job teaches us is that perseverance will pay off. Job also teaches that if you position yourself in God's will and you wait this thing out, you will discover what Job discovered. You will discover that God has already worked it out. So many people get ahead of God's timing by being anxious because they are nervous, or impatient, but the Bible says be anxious for nothing, but in all things by prayer and supplication, let your requests be made known unto God.

Job makes a request to God and then he takes a stand or position of FAITH in God. Perhaps that is what God is saying to someone today who is big on the *request side* but suffering on the *stand side.* You cannot ask God to 'do' if you refuse to believe. Your convictions must be clear. Your stance must be sure. Your resolve must be resounding. In the midst of any situation, it is important to develop a "FAITH in God posture." You must look and speak like God, and you have got to believe God no matter what it looks like. You must tell folk on the other side of that darkroom door, that no matter what they say about your negative situation, God is still working this thing out. The question should never be if God is going to do it. You are not reading this devotional because you wonder if God is going to do it. You have a history with God. You know He has an impeccable track record. You have seen God do too much over the years to even let doubt come out of your mouth. Deep down inside, you know God is going to do it. The real question is how long are you willing to wait for God to manifest it into your life? I know it is tough but wait it out. I know you are pushed to the edge but wait it out. If you wait this thing out, God will work it out.

What does today's Faith Workout Devotion teach you about taking a posture of faith?

WORKOUT REFLECTIONS

DAY
8
15 KG
FAITH
WORKOUT

DAY 8
FAITH WORKOUT

I want to ask you a personal question today. Can God put His reputation on the line with you? If God's reputation was based on how you respond in your darkroom experience, what would be the end result? We have got to be willing to expect and respect the will of God. God might not do what we want Him to do but we must acknowledge His sovereignty. God's Sovereignty is His "absolute right to do all things according to His own pleasure." God offered up Job to Satan without asking his permission. God will never ask for your permission to put you in the darkroom to develop your faith because He knows that you would say no. He knows you would say things like, "Why me Lord? I got a neighbor across the street that doesn't even go to church!"

Know that God is a good, good Father. God knew Job's potential before He knew it himself. If you are in a valley of the shadow of death, God will be there with you.

Job 1:12 KJV – "And the LORD said unto Satan, Behold, all that he hath is in thy power; only upon him put not forth thine hand. So Satan went forth from the presence of the LORD."

God says that Satan could not touch Job's body. God rations out the trial. On the surface, it will appear that the devil is in charge. When the Darkroom door is closed, the devil will think he is in charge. The devil couldn't go after Job without permission from God. You can praise God right now! If Satan had to have permission, then his territory must be limited.

What does today's Faith Workout Devotion teach you about God's Sovereignty?

WORKOUT REFLECTIONS

DAY
9
15 KG
FAITH
WORKOUT

DAY 9
FAITH WORKOUT

After the matriarch of the Griffin family (Mother Eara Mae Griffin) transitioned to Heaven, as a pastor, I experienced a spirit of heaviness for months. I wasn't just grieving; I felt upset at God and confused. I just couldn't wrap my finite mind around the fact that I had prayed for hundreds of people and watched God heal them in many of my revival services. I've seen the miracle-working power of God; I'm a miracle myself because God supernaturally healed me from a severe speech impediment from my childhood. My state of confusion lingered because my disappointment and pain wouldn't allow me to see past God's sovereignty. Nobody knew what was going on in my head, not even my precious wife. My thoughts became frozen in time because of my pain.

What's going on in your head? I submit to you today that even pastors and members of their congregation of all sizes and make-ups are committing suicide, losing their marriages, stressing out over darkroom experiences, and leaving ministry altogether. Many times, the crisis can be averted if only the church would become a place where people could honestly confess their thoughts to another without being judged.

What's going on in your head matters to me and it matters to God. I'm more and more convinced as I speak with people on a daily basis that the pressure people are feeling in the darkroom is real. It's affecting them and those whom they love to some extent.

What do you do when God's sovereignty overrides your expectations, plans, and feelings? This darkroom experience was one of the darkest seasons in my life. I experienced loss, hurt, pain, confusion, and frustration. It was during this darkroom experience that God spoke to me from His Word. **In 2 Timothy 2:13 (AMPC) it reads,**

"If we are faithless {do not believe and are untrue to Him}, He remains true (faithful to His Word and His righteous character), for He cannot deny Himself."

So, amid our darkroom experiences, God is faithful. **God is---Faithful**, loyal, reliable, on point accurate, and trustworthy (or worthy of trust). He can fulfill promises or impossible obligations. Faithful means His reputation is impeccable with a perfect track record.

What does today's Faith Workout Devotion teach you about addressing what is going on in your head?

WORKOUT REFLECTIONS

DAY
10
15 KG
FAITH
WORKOUT

DAY 10
FAITH WORKOUT

Faith is the prescription for abundant living. When used as prescribed by a doctor, prescription medicines can be helpful in treating many illnesses.

As Christians, our life depends on the development and condition of our faith in God. That's what Paul spoke of in Hebrews 10:38. He said, "Now the just shall live by faith…" in other words, faith is the prescription for an abundant life.

Have you ever read God's hall of fame in Hebrews chapter 11? These men and women of faith did miraculous things, who through faith subdued kingdoms, wrought righteousness, obtained promises, stopped the mouths of lions. And how did they do it? FAITH!

"And others had trial of cruel mockings and scourgings, yea, moreover of bonds and imprisonment: They were stoned, they were sawn asunder, were tempted, were slain with the sword: And these all, having obtained a good report through faith, received not the promise:" (Hebrews 11:36-37, 39 KJV)

Listen to this revelation! Some had FAITH to *escape*; some had FAITH to *endure*. What if it is God's will for you to endure instead of escaping?

Will God be enough if He allows you to go into the fiery furnace of affliction?

What does today's Faith Workout Devotion teach you about God's perfect will for your life?

WORKOUT REFLECTIONS

DAY
11
15 KG
FAITH
WORKOUT

DAY 11
FAITH WORKOUT

Optimism or pessimism will be a decision you must make alone in your darkroom experiences.

Proverbs 17:22 NKJV – "A merry heart does good, like medicine, but a broken spirit dries the bones."

Proverbs 17:22 NLT – "A cheerful heart is good medicine, but a broken spirit saps a person's strength."

How you view your darkroom experiences has a lot to do with how you go through it. For some people, all they see is the negative. You cannot be a person that is always being fed negativism. These are people who do not expect any good things in life, they only see the bad things or have a skeptical view of life.

An optimist is a person who tends to be hopeful and confident about the future or success of something. They believe that good must ultimately prevail over evil. They see things from a hope perspective, the glass is half full type of person.

Pessimist is a person who tends to see the worst aspect of things or believes that the worst will happen. They believe that evil will always prevail over good. They see the glass half empty. An optimist understands that dark seasons can be difficult, but at least they have hope—earnest expectation. There has to be an effort to be intentional. You have to stay positive in this season. This is about your perspective. Your perspective is the way you see or view something. Whether that something is your business, marriage, finances, or life. The word perspective has a Latin root meaning "*look through*" or "perceive," and all the meanings of the word perspective have something to do with looking. You cannot have a perspective that is too hot or too cold. You have to be a thermostat because a thermostat perspective can change the environment. It will be your thoughts, feelings, and actions while in the darkroom that will determine your perspective.

What does today's Faith Workout Devotion teach you about Optimism vs Pessimism?

WORKOUT REFLECTIONS

DAY
12
15 KG
FAITH
WORKOUT

DAY 12
FAITH WORKOUT

Today, have the maturity to encourage yourself.

Jeremiah 20:9 NIV – "But if I say, "I will not mention his word or speak anymore in his name," his word is in my heart like a fire, a fire shut up in my bones. I am weary of holding it in; indeed, I cannot."

Jeremiah didn't want to do it another day. He was done. Have you ever said to yourself and others "I'm done!" Jeremiah matured to the point that the Word called him back to himself.

Job had to encourage himself. Job went through one darkroom experience after another. He kept receiving bad news one after another. There are going to be times when you will have to will yourself to praise and worship God.

Job 1:20-22 NIV – "At this, Job got up and tore his robe and shaved his head. Then he fell to the ground in worship and said: "Naked I came from my mother's womb, and naked I will depart. The Lord gave and the Lord has taken away; may the name of the Lord be praised." In all this, Job did not sin by charging God with wrongdoing." Job matured to the place that he reverted back to what he always knew. Job worshipped God!

Job 13:15 NIV – "Though he slay me, yet will I hope in him; I will surely defend my ways to his face." They may call him insane, but Job made up his mind to put his trust in God. You don't ever have to feel guilty about removing negative or toxic people from your life. It doesn't matter whether someone is a co-worker, family member or even church member. You don't have to allow people to invade your personal space with negative energy. It's one thing if a person owns up to their negative behavior and makes an effort to change. But if not, "protect your spirit" and encourage yourself.

What does today's Faith Workout Devotion teach you about encouraging yourself?

WORKOUT REFLECTIONS

DAY
13
15 KG
FAITH
WORKOUT

DAY 13
FAITH WORKOUT

One writer said: Life is like a camera—focus on what's important.

So many times, when we are going through a darkroom experience, we have the tendency of losing focus. Darkness has a way of causing many people to focus on their loss instead of what is important. The things that you value most in life will be where your focus and priorities lie.

In the Bible, David had to trust God. Saul tried to kill David and David had to learn something about staying focused on what is important.

Psalm 23:4 NIV – "Even though I walk through the darkest valley, I will fear no evil, for you are with me; your rod and your staff, they comfort me." You are not in the valley or darkroom experience by yourself.

We have a divine partnership which makes up our optimism. To come back from Ziklag and see that all had been destroyed; the family had been kidnapped and people have turned against you, this is exceedingly difficult to endure. Know that no matter what, you will recover all.

I Samuel 30:6 NKJV – "Now David was greatly distressed, for the people spoke of stoning him, because the soul of all the people was grieved, every man for his sons and his daughters. But David strengthened himself in the Lord his

God." David had a spirit of optimism. David asked God what to do. God told him to get up and go back. Know that even in your darkest moments, you shall recover all.

Make this confession of faith to yourself, "I shall recover all." I will not focus on what I have lost. The way you survive this season is to stay FOCUSED. Let nothing separate you from the love of Jesus Christ.

In all the bad news, know that He is good news!

What does today's Faith Workout Devotion teach you about staying Focus?

WORKOUT REFLECTIONS

DAY
14
15 KG
FAITH
WORKOUT

DAY 14
FAITH WORKOUT

In Ecclesiastes chapter 3 verse 1 it reads, "***To everything, there is a season, and a time to every purpose under the heaven:***"

Crossing the bridges of life is a collection series of entrances and exits. All entrances and exits experience pressure. If we were to consider these darkroom experiences in the physical, just think about childbirth for a moment, there is pressure on both the mother and the baby. The baby is exiting the womb and entering the world to begin its new life. The mother however is ending the provision of the womb for the baby and she is entering motherhood.

We experience the same thing spiritually, emotionally, and sometimes physically while in the darkroom. With exiting and entering comes new seasons, challenges, graces, and the development of our faith. I received an unexpected phone call one day. I was asked by a ministry leader, Pastor Darryl, how are you dealing with this pandemic? I shared with him and others that I've learned a valuable lesson.

"ATTITUDE IS IMPORTANT" – Our attitude is what influences all our actions. It is only the positive attitude which gets us good results. It is critical in life to finish what you have started whether you are EXITING or ENTERING new chapters of your life.

We all experience pressure while in the darkroom. But the test for us is how we handle these circumstances and situations when God turns the lights out. We can choose God's divine plan and respond accordingly to the Fruit of the Spirit, or we can react through our flesh and emotions. We will, at some point and time, meet the same darkroom experiences again if we do not submit totally to His plan. Remember, the key is "ATTITUDE"- maintaining a positive attitude while surviving this new normal. So do not stand on the bridge with one foot between the exit and the entrance. **A double-minded person will receive nothing from the Lord.**

What does today's Faith Workout Devotion teach you about entering or exiting new chapters of life?

WORKOUT REFLECTIONS

DAY
15
15 KG
FAITH
WORKOUT

DAY 15
FAITH WORKOUT

"But we have this treasure in earthen vessels, that the excellence of the power may be of God, and not of us." (2 Corinthians 4:7 KJV)

"We are like clay jars in which this treasure is stored. The real power comes from God and not from us." (2 Corinthians 4:7 CEV)

The first thing that Apostle Paul tells us in 2 Corinthians 4:7-12 is that sometimes life will throw us blows that we are not able to handle on our own. And contrary to popular belief, you are not as strong as you think. He says that we are fragile clay pots: mass-produced, ordinary containers that do not amount to very much. We are fragile and ordinary, even the most impressive of us. What do you do when God thrusts you into the darkroom without any warning? Vs 8 & 9 says he was afflicted but not restricted, baffled but not to the point of despair, abused but not abandoned, knocked down but not terminated; literally knocked down, but still standing.

Why did Paul not give up? I don't think it was because Paul was naturally optimistic or persistent. I think it was because Paul realized that his suffering had a purpose.

The thing that keeps me up at night sometimes is wondering if the suffering that my wife and I have gone through was worth it. Paul tells us here that it was worth it. It is worth it because your darkroom experiences can accomplish at least two things: **God uses your weakness to show His glory—** Your weakness is a great backdrop to demonstrate the power of God. (Vs 7)

God uses your sufferings to advance His gospel (Vs 10, 15). ***"For it is all for your sake, so that as grace extends to more and more people it may increase thanksgiving, to the glory of God." (2 Corinthians 4:15 ESV)*** Our suffering is a prerequisite for the spreading of the gospel. It mirrors the crucifix pattern of the gospel: life comes through death.

Are you an open vessel or a closed vessel? An open vessel can contain an unending amount, but if the vessel is closed it is limited. To contain that which is greater than oneself is to remain an open vessel. Unfortunately, many people have become closed vessels and are limiting God. We have treasure (translated storehouse for precious things, a deposit of wealth) in earthen vessels but must remain open to God and His limitless nature. If we don't remain open, we limit ourselves to our finite understanding. We are to continue to grow in our faith and remain open vessels during dark seasons.

What does today's Faith Workout Devotion teach you about open or closed vessels?

WORKOUT REFLECTIONS

DAY
16
15 KG
FAITH
WORKOUT

DAY 16
FAITH WORKOUT

Being a champion is about having a certain mindset. It is about approaching life victoriously. It is an attitude of confidence. There is a certain way people walk when they know God. They walk as Champions. They realize that nothing is too difficult as long as they have God in their lives.

"And he said, the things which are impossible with men are possible with God." (Luke 18:27 KJV)

Jesus said to him, "If you can believe, all things are possible to him who believes." (Mark 9:23 NKJV)

A champion (from the Latin origin-campio) is the victor in a challenge, contest, or competition who has surpassed all rivals in a competition and won. We are champions!

We look at challenging circumstances and think we do not have the time or resources to overcome them. How can we overcome the loss of a job, a failed marriage, a diagnosis that has taken away your health or threatens our future plans?

The things we go through in our darkroom experiences have little to do with us and everything to do with God. We have got to remember, even though we cannot do it, God can! With God, all things are possible. "I can do all things through Christ which strengtheneth me." (Phil. 4:13 KJV)

Man's extremity is God's opportunity. One translation of Phil. 4:13 GNT tells us, ***"We have the strength to face all conditions by the power that Christ gives us."***

We must realize that God would not put us in front of something that He did not feel we could achieve. If He put you in front of it, then He knew you could achieve it, so it really comes down to our own mindset. Champions see things as they should be no matter what tangible things are in front of them. What is even more amazing is the ability to visualize something on the inside of you that has not yet manifested on the outside. Today it is about your MIND-SET.

What does today's Faith Workout Devotion teach you about being a faith champion?

WORKOUT REFLECTIONS

DAY
17
15 KG
FAITH
WORKOUT

DAY 17

FAITH WORKOUT

The great American hero, Dr. Martin Luther King Jr., who was a man of passive resistance, always condemned violence. He said, "Faith is taking the first step even when you don't see the whole staircase." He took giant leaps of faith in the dark and changed the fabric of America, which still has resounding effects today.

It's easy to have the faith of a giant when money is in the bank, doors of opportunities are plentiful, and everyone is healthy and happy. But faith is tested and tried when the journey grows dark with uncertainty and there is no glimpse of light.

To be a faith champion, you need a strong belief system in God.

"But without faith it is impossible to please him: for he that cometh to God must believe that he is, and that he is a rewarder of them that diligently seek him." (Hebrews 11:6 KJV)

Without faith, it is impossible to please God. We have got to believe God can do it before He does it. We have to visualize ourselves winning, conquering, succeeding, and living a victorious life for Christ.

Michael Jordan, called the GOAT by many people, had a coach that made the whole team visualize winning before they actually played the game. It was told that Michael and his teammates always believed that this played a large part in them winning so often. Michael Jordan adopted this winning concept for himself and as a result, he became one of the most notorious basketball players of all time. We need to adopt this habit as well. We need to visualize ourselves coming out of our darkroom situations before God actually brings us out. It is all about visualization while you are in the Darkroom.

What does today's Faith Workout Devotion teach you about visualization?

WORKOUT REFLECTIONS

DAY
18
15 KG
FAITH
WORKOUT

DAY 18
FAITH WORKOUT

Apostle Paul pointed out something remarkably interesting in ***Galatians 6:9 KJV – "And let us not be weary in well doing: for in due season we shall reap, if we faint not."***

Are you weary of serving in ministry? Ministry burnout is all too common. My wife, Lenora, and I have served in ministry since I accepted my calling in 1984. Although serving in the ministry is a good thing, I'm not against it but many find themselves stretched too thin. They have never found a balance between ministry and family.

When we are stretched thin in every area of our life, the first thing we do is stop serving in ministry. We have too much going on and we need balance in our life.

Is it possible that the things that are out of order in our personal lives, are being carried over in ministry?

It is very evident that when frustration is present, it is usually a sign that our priorities are out of order. Think of it this way, when things are not right at home, what is your attitude and behavior like when you show up at church or work to serve?

My wife and I have made a very conscious decision to remember God's priorities while facing Darkroom experiences which are: God, spouse, family, ministry, and work. And your first ministry begins at home. Therefore, if your home life is in chaos, it is not time to quit serving, it is time to deal with the root of the chaos at home.

In fact, having things in order at home is only one part, knowing where you should be serving is another. Sometimes frustration occurs while serving, because we are serving where we do not have the grace in that area of ministry. Please don't misunderstand, there are seasons when we have to serve in areas of ministry where there is a need. And I believe in those times; if it is for you, the grace will be on you to do it. But you will only reap a due season if you faint not.

What does today's Faith Workout Devotion teach you about not growing weary?

WORKOUT REFLECTIONS

DAY
19
15 KG
FAITH
WORKOUT

DAY 19
FAITH WORKOUT

Like many, there are times during dark seasons we grow weary. Not because we do not want to serve God or feel stretched in serving His people; but because we don't see the results we want. Listen! I've been there! In my own life, I must confess I just didn't see the results I wanted.

However, when we read Hebrews 6:10 in the Amplified translation, it should bless and encourage you. This verse has become part of my daily confession of faith and devotion that I have it written down in my office. I wrote it down to keep it before my eyes that I would remind myself not to grow weary in serving.

"For God is not unrighteous to forget or overlook your labor and the love which you have shown for His names' sake in ministering to the needs of the saints (His own consecrated people), as you still do." (Hebrew 6:10 AMPC)

Amazing! What a promise from God that we can hold onto during darkroom experiences. Especially during times of doubt or fear regarding our purpose, and in our serving while waiting for our due season.

God is aware of the time and emotional energy we have invested to serve His kingdom. Yes, I'm a living witness that our God is mindful of the time, emotional energy, prayers, love, servanthood attitude, patience and even money, we have invested in others.

Hebrews 6:10 tells us today that our God will never overlook what we have done. So, as we invest time, energy, and money sacrificially we have peace knowing, without a shadow of doubt, that our faithful God will reward us. Therefore, we refuse to grow weary, tired, give way, relinquish our faith nor give into discouragement. Giving up is not an option, as we will keep pressing forward with joy to do what God has called us to do, until He says we have completed our assignment. Stand firm on this declaration of FAITH no matter how dark it seems. God has not forgotten!

What does today's Faith Workout Devotion teach you about "God has not forgotten?"

WORKOUT REFLECTIONS

DAY
20
15 KG
FAITH
WORKOUT

DAY 20
FAITH WORKOUT

In my book, "Faith Developed in the Darkroom", I share my Darkroom experience in chapter 4 which is titled "Doubters Are Welcome". I described the time when my wife, Lenora, and I was dealing with extreme financial hardship.

I remember this narrative like it was yesterday. One morning in my hotel room while preparing a revival message in Gary, IN, I received a call from one of my neighbors back in Atlanta, GA. He sounded extremely nervous but then proceeded to tell me that the DeKalb County's Sheriffs were at my house taking all our possession to the street. We were facing eviction and my wife was at work and didn't know what was happening.

I asked God, "Why is this happening to us? I am out here doing your will, how could You let this happen?" I felt confused, embarrassed, and my heart was heavy. I began to doubt God. I asked Him, "Where are You when we need You?" We didn't understand. In my hotel room, I fluctuated between anxiety and frustration.

It seemed as though the Lord had taken everything away from us, for no conclusive reason.

Do you not know that you can be in God's perfect will and still experience financial hardship or various kinds of loss?

The suffering we endure today equips us for tomorrow's ministry. When we faithfully follow and trust in the Lord, we learn how to develop a spirit of endurance while waiting in the darkroom. That endurance produces godly character. With that character, we can respond to every darkroom experience with contentment, gratitude, and joy. If you find yourself in the midst of seemingly insurmountable circumstances today, put your faith in God's Word for strength and hope.

"My friends, consider yourselves fortunate when all kinds of trials come your way, for you know that when your faith succeeds in facing such trials, the result is the ability to endure. Make sure that your endurance carries you all the way without failing, so that you may be perfect and complete, lacking nothing." (James 1: 2-4 GNTD)

What does today's Faith Workout Devotion teach you about endurance?

WORKOUT REFLECTIONS

DAY
21
15 KG
FAITH
WORKOUT

DAY 21
FAITH WORKOUT

What we need in the Darkroom is patience in God's sovereignty. Patience is the spiritual ability to endure dark seasons and difficult circumstances; it is perseverance in face of delay.

"If a man die, shall he live again? all the days of my appointed time will I wait, till my change come." (Job 14:14 KJV)

If a person has been as sick as you, can they be well again? If a person has credit as bad as yours, can they get back on financial track? If a person has been wounded, can they ever trust again? Some of you are in your afterlife season now. We are living our best life right now. You have died so to speak and have been brought back. Some of us can be witnesses that you can come back bigger and better.

There is a collision between Chronos and Kairos time. When Job says, "all the days of my appointed time" he is referring to it as the collision between the two times (Chronos and Kairos). You can leave at 8 a.m. to arrive on time for a 9 o'clock appointment. This is Chronos. You get there at 9 o'clock and they say, "sit down". You know your appointment is at 9 o'clock, but they tell you to sit down. Your time is not guaranteed. You are just in position. You notice that there are several people there that have a 9 o'clock appointment as well. You got to find comfort in knowing:

The doctor is there. The doctor is in the building. You must find comfort in the fact that there are people leaving the doctor's office who have already seen the doctor. There are people still waiting to see him. You have to wait, be patient until your change comes. Stay in position, because eventually they will call your name and eventually your situation will change. If you get up and leave, you might miss what the doctor has for you. Therefore, we have to submit to the doctor's time. Wait until your change comes. I know it is hard to wait in dark seasons for many of us. But when you wait patiently, there has got to be no doubt that your situation is coming to pass as long as you are in position. Today keep in your mind, a change is going to come.

What does today's Faith Workout Devotion teach you about waiting until your change comes?

WORKOUT REFLECTIONS

DAY
22
15 KG
FAITH
WORKOUT

DAY 22
FAITH WORKOUT

Romans 10:17 KJV – "So then faith cometh by hearing, and hearing by the word of God."

Today God has given to every believer faith to fight for your family. There is a cry in the earth realm concerning broken marriages, sibling rivalry, teenage rebellion, crumbling families. We are told there is nothing we can do to restore what we once had. They say our defense is weak against the wiles of the enemy—the devil—and warned that he will infiltrate the very existence of our lives and the lives of our loved ones. NEVERTHELESS…the Bible says that if you will fight for your family when it seems dark, *"Our God will fight for us." (Nehemiah 4:13-14,20)*

There is a cause that is worth your fighting for and that is the protection of your family. If the home is the number one priority of the devil, then we better make sure it is the number one priority in our lives. You better be committed to God and you better be committed to your marriage and your family. If this is a weak area, then the enemy will make himself right at home and divide and conquer your family. Be mindful that we have a strong and mighty God, and the Bible promises that *"No weapon formed against us will prosper."* We have the God of victory in the home that is built upon Christ the solid Rock.

Do not wait, DO IT NOW—Be aware of dangerous distractions that can take you and your family away at critical times when your family needs to be in the Word and be in the house of God. There is no better time than RIGHT NOW to reconstruct, rebuild and fight for your "family."

Everyone is busy with daily commitments. Where do you see your priorities today? Do they need to change? Do they put God and family first?

What does today's Faith Workout Devotion teach you about faith for your family?

WORKOUT REFLECTIONS

DAY
23
15 KG
FAITH
WORKOUT

DAY 23
FAITH WORKOUT

God is a God of restoration. Seasons of chaos and darkroom experiences are unavoidable in life. These dark seasons can make you feel as if all is lost and abandoned because the wreckage of what is left from the storm can feel daunting and beyond repair. The beauty of your personal relationship with Christ is that He not only is the Lord of restoration, but He is the God of making all things new in Him.

Throughout the scriptures, it is clear that when God seeks to restore, compassion is coupled along with that intention. Jeremiah 33:26 says, ***"For I will restore their fortunes and have compassion on them."*** It is God's heart for His chosen people to not only be restored but to compassionately restore something even better than before.

May God remind you this day that He is working all things together for His glory, and for your benefit (Romans 8:28). May you have the courage and strength to stand in faith that He will honor these promises to you in His timing and way, and that in His compassionate love, we have all that we will ever need. We have life and life more abundantly.

God is the God of restoration and compassion. Come before Him today with hands open to what He will do. God will not only restore but make better than all you could ever ask for or imagine and be the Giver of all good things.

What does today's Faith Workout Devotion teach you about restoration?

WORKOUT REFLECTIONS

DAY
24
15 KG
FAITH
WORKOUT

DAY 24
FAITH WORKOUT

It's important to know that our period of development in the darkroom may take longer than someone else's. It's possible that someone else may occupy the darkroom while class is in session.

Job 23:10 AMP states, "But He knows the way that I take [and He pays attention to it]. When He has tried me, I will come forth as [refined] gold [pure and luminous]."

Sometimes, God will delay His answer and we are left wondering why He is so reluctant to intervene in our affairs. If we are not careful, looking at someone else's season of development can create bitterness and resentment.

Bitterness is the product of intense animosity, characterized by ill will. Resentment is indignant displeasure which results from a wrong, an insult or injury, either real, imagined, or unintentional.

A classic case of "hold a grudge and get even" syndrome is found in the story of Cain and Abel (Genesis 4:1-16). Cain was angry because his offering was not accepted while his brother's offering was accepted. It really was not a matter between Cain and Abel at all, but between Cain and God, for it was God who had rejected Cain's offering. But Cain became resentful and depressed. Instead of repenting and asking forgiveness of the Lord, he turned on his brother.

How many times do we look at our brother or sister with distain because we are in the darkroom and they are on the outside door of the darkroom?

Professional counselors reveal that a large percentage of those being counseled today are angry, embittered, and resentful towards others. Bottled-up-feelings can eat away until some people become emotionally crippled and physically ill.

Their ability to function is impaired, diminishing their effectiveness. Some become so obsessed with the urge to "get even" that their personal relationships, both within and without the family begins to erode. As you detect resentment and bitterness in your heart, treat it as sin. God's Word says, ***"Put off all these: anger, wrath, malice, blasphemy, filthy language." (Colossians 3:8 NKJV)***

What does today's Faith Workout Devotion teach you about dealing with bitterness and resentment?

WORKOUT REFLECTIONS

DAY
25
15 KG
FAITH
WORKOUT

DAY 25

FAITH WORKOUT

I believe today that someone reading this devotional said: Lord I'm at my breaking point! If something or someone has reached their **breaking point,** they have so many problems or dark moments that they can no longer cope with them and may soon collapse or be unable to continue walking in faith. However, learning how to overcome your breaking point is crucial to your faith journey.

When you reach your breaking point, you need spiritual tools to help you release. No, I don't mean making a strawberry smoothie but, if it helps, go for it. I'm talking about a good old-fashioned faith workout.

Jesus gives us some spiritual tools in the book of Matthew that says, ***"Come to Me, all you who labor and are heavy laden, and I will give you rest. Take My yoke upon you and learn from Me, for I am gentle and lowly in heart, and you will find rest for your souls. For My yoke is easy, and My burden is light." (Matthew 11:28-30 NKJV)***

Breaking point is the point or moment in your darkroom experience where you reach your max point as it relates to things you can handle. In human psychology, the breaking point is a moment of stress in which a person breaks down or a situation becomes critical.

When you receive a foreclosure notice in the mail, this is an example of a breaking point. When the marriage is at the peak of divorce, or there is no relief to your health issues, or when no financial aid has come and it is time to start class, this is an example of a breaking point. Before something has reached its "breaking point," it has undergone many tests, trials, and tensions. Finally, pressure has built up so much that something must give way.

All of us have experienced dark moments where our faith has been pushed to the edge. God is sending you this word today to let you know that your breaking point is about being closer to Him. Know that whatever is challenging your faith, will not be the end and it won't be the end of you. In verse 28 Jesus said, **"Come to me, all you who labor and are heavy laden, and I will give you rest."** Rest mentioned in verse 28 implies support and exchange. In other words, give it to Him and our God who is stronger and wiser will offer to ease your load so you may enjoy His rest.

What does today's Faith Workout Devotion teach you about "breaking point moments?"

WORKOUT REFLECTIONS

DAY
26
15 KG
FAITH
WORKOUT

DAY 26
FAITH WORKOUT

Immediately after declaring that He is "the door" in John 10:11, Jesus declares **"I am the good shepherd."** He describes Himself as not only "the shepherd" but the "good shepherd." A good shepherd that not only protects, guides, and nurtures His flock but seeks us as well. Ancient shepherds had a remedy for sheep that would continue to leave the sheepfold and stray away. The shepherds would break the straying lamb's leg and then splint it so the lamb would be totally dependent on the shepherd and learn not to stray away again. God says, I want to break your leg when you stray away from My divine will, but I know how to break you. I'll use calamity, hardship, crushing, breakups, or even financial ruin to get your attention and break you.

Rest is available for those who are ready. Are you ready? You have got to get to a place in your life where you are willing to allow God to do what is necessary to destress you.

David was acquainted with stress. He got a revelation. He realized that the Lord was his good shepherd. He realized that the Lord would make him lie down in green pastures. When God is ready for you to rest, He will make you rest. Whether it is voluntary or involuntary, you will rest. **Waiting on God involves being at rest in the Lord.**

When you lie down and rest, God will restore and refresh you. Too many of us are trying to get restored on the run.

Sometimes God has to treat you like a car that is not running properly. He has to put you in the auto repair shop and jack you up, so He can take a good look at the problem under the hood. There is a little control freak in all of us. But when you are ready to relinquish control, God will step in. David shared his testimony in ***Psalm 23:2-3 NKJV – "He makes me to lie down in green pastures; He leads me beside the still waters. He restores my soul; He leads me in the paths of righteousness For His name's sake."***

What does today's Faith Workout Devotion teach me about Jesus the Good Shepherd?

WORKOUT REFLECTIONS

DAY
27
15 KG
FAITH
WORKOUT

DAY 27

FAITH WORKOUT

Nothing compares to the contentment of the Creator. God desires for your contentment with Him to grow. No matter how many "good things" we are blessed with that gives us contentment, nothing compares to the contentment you receive from God. Contentment is not something that's found; it is an attitude that comes from knowing you are in God's perfect will. We need contentment to endure darkroom experiences.

"Now godliness with contentment is great gain." **(I Timothy 6:6 NKJV)** Stop living your life to impress others and learn to impress God. What is contentment and how is it attained? Contentment, contrary to popular belief, does not mean being satisfied where you are. Rather, it is knowing God's plan for your life, having a conviction to live it, and believing that God's peace is greater than the world's problems.

"Therefore we also, since we are surrounded by so great a cloud of witnesses, let us lay aside every weight, and the sin which so easily ensnares us, and let us run with endurance the race that is set before us." (Hebrews 12:1 NKJV) I have my own race to run. So, I must learn to stay focused and run in my own lane.

God is trying to work things out in your life, but you keep looking to everyone else for the answer to your darkroom experiences. This is how many Christians get trapped into a discontented life by adopting worldly goals: more, bigger, and best. The Bible identifies these as indulgence, greed, pride. If we are not careful after being in the Darkroom any length of time, after a while there is a tendency to fall back into the same old habit of desiring and getting more, rationalizing that somehow it is "serving the Lord." This is evidence of a lack of peace, a lack of spiritual growth, and a growing doubt about God's ability to provide.

Thankfulness is needed while in the darkroom. Thankfulness is a state of mind, not an accumulation of things. Until you can truly thank God for what you have and be willing to accept God's provision—contentment and perfect will for your life—contentment will never be possible.

What does today's Faith Workout Devotion teach you about contentment?

WORKOUT REFLECTIONS

DAY
28
15 KG
FAITH
WORKOUT

DAY 28
FAITH WORKOUT

Floods, racial injustice, political division, economic poverty, and even learning how to deal with this pandemic are things we can run into. What I run to can keep me alive. What we need today is a desire for the living God. This is the season to run to God. Water represents our source of strength. The body cannot live without water and in the same manner, the soul cannot live without the presence of God.

John 4:14 NKJV says, "But whoever drinks of the water that I shall give him will never thirst. But the water that I shall give him will become in him a fountain of water springing up into everlasting life."

Some people are thirsty, and they think they can go around on just a **drip** instead of a **drink.** What happens when you dehydrate? I've experienced dehydration once or twice in my life. I remember lying on the couch feeling lightheaded, thirsty, tired and had a very dry mouth. I felt like I was leaving this world. By the time you feel thirsty, your body is already dehydrated. Our thirst lags behind our actual level of hydration.

May I ask you a question? Are you thirsty? In fact, when you are thirsty, you could already be dehydrated, having lost as much as one to two percent of your body's water content. And with that kind of water loss, you may start to experience cognitive impairments like stress, agitation, and hallucinations. With all the things you are dealing with, a sip is not going to get it. The Lord does not need you being thirsty. Jesus said: **"Blessed are those who hunger and thirst for righteousness, for they will be filled."** (Matthew 5:6 CSB)

Thirst, for what is real will lead to being filled!

You can't expect people or things to quench your thirst. We think people and things can fulfill it for us and we are disappointed every time. Only God can quench that thirst. In this day and time, we think tangible stuff makes us fulfilled. It is not the things that money can buy it is the things money cannot buy. If I focus on the things that money cannot buy, then if I lose everything, I have through a darkroom experience, I won't lose my mind, because I know where my fulfillment comes from. I am a witness that God will give to you in a way that you won't need again. You are about to embark on a season where you won't need for anything. When God becomes our fulfillment, we don't have wants, because our faith is in God our source.

What does today's Faith Workout Devotion teach you about having a thirst for God?

WORKOUT REFLECTIONS

DAY
29
15 KG
FAITH
WORKOUT

DAY 29
FAITH WORKOUT

The devil is very clever when it comes to our faith. Let me share with you what he once did to me when I was at my darkest moment. He may try to do the same old thing to you. He will start agreeing with you so he can trip you up.

He will whisper suggestive thoughts in your mind and say, "Sure, you are saved by faith in Christ. But how do you know that your faith is good enough or strong enough to sustain you while waiting on God. What if your faith is too weak? What if you don't make it out of this darkroom alive?" He tried to make me put my faith in my faith, rather than my faith in Christ and His Word.

Superman is almost unstoppable. Notice I said "almost" because he does have one vulnerability. You have seen the movies, Kryptonite weakens him, and too much of it can destroy him.

Unbelief is our kryptonite. Even those mature believers with faith in God struggle with doubt on occasion and say like the man in Mark's gospel, chapter 9:24, "***The father instantly cried out, I do believe, but help me overcome my unbelief!" (NLT)***

Many people think doubt is the opposite of faith, but it is not. Unbelief is the opposite of faith. Unbelief refers to a willful refusal to believe, while doubt refers to inner uncertainty. (Psalm 78:17-19)

Some Christians think doubt is unforgivable, but it is not. God does not condemn us when we question Him. Both Job and David repeatedly questioned God, but they were not condemned. God is big enough to handle all our doubts and all our questions. So, today I release you now to ask God any question you desire.

What does today's Faith Workout Devotion teach you about overcoming unbelief?

WORKOUT REFLECTIONS

DAY
30
15 KG
FAITH
WORKOUT

DAY 30
FAITH WORKOUT

How can we turn our faith towards God and sing His praises when we are facing dark moments? Where do we find words of praise and thanksgiving when our heart is full of sorrow and struggle? How can we develop faith in God who gives us different answers than what we pray for, who only shows a side of Himself when we look back over our lives, and Who allows us to walk in darkness for months (and sometimes years) at a time?

In Psalm 34, David reminds us that we should praise God through the good times and bad. Praise should fill our hearts every day, no matter our circumstances—especially when we are facing dark seasons.

Psalm 34:1-4 NIV – "I will extol the Lord at all times; his praise will always be on my lips. I will glory in the Lord; let the afflicted hear and rejoice. Glorify the Lord with me; let us exalt his name together. I sought the Lord, and he answered me; he delivered me from all my fears."

When you feel claustrophobic in the darkroom, fight your battles with praise. *When* the pressure begins to close in, you may find yourself without the words to say, unable to find those words of prayer. When I don't have the words to pray, I turn to verses in God's Word about praising God and use those to pray through God's Word. Start somewhere. Praise Him in the darkroom, with a Bible verse of praise, a prewritten prayer, or even a worship song. Learn how to lean on the words of others until you find your own. Make a conscious decision to lift up your praise. One of the things the enemy wants to do is to get you to isolate yourself so he can silence your praise. Get your own party hat and encourage yourself. Start looking and sounding like you have been lifted out of it. Now, how do we do this? We ought to give God praise for all that He has done for us! Declare that I may get discouraged, but I will never lose my praise. I will not let my situation change my relationship with the one that can change my situation. Know that when you lift Him up, He will lift you up!

I pray today you'll be encouraged and take hope in God's power, even as the battles seem to close in around you. Remember that God is surrounding you!

What does today's Faith Workout Devotion teach you about praising God?

WORKOUT REFLECTIONS

ABOUT THE AUTHOR

Darryl O. Griffin, D. Div.

In 1984, he heard the Lord speak to him in an audible voice, "Go ye into all the world and preach the gospel to every creature." From that moment until now, the burden of lost souls has been his purpose and responsibility of spreading the gospel message far and near. He holds a Masters of Christian Counseling (Family Counseling & Leadership emphasis) from Midwest Seminary of Bible Theology and a Doctor of Divinity from St. Thomas University, Jacksonville FL.

Dr. Darryl O. Griffin is known as a relevant expositor of God's word in evangelical circles and is unique for having the ability to communicate complex theological truths through simplistic yet profound, revelation.

Darryl is a born polymath. He conducts leadership seminars, he is a conference speaker, and senior pastor of Believer's Choice Life Church, in Memphis TN.

Darryl is historically the first African American pastor to serve on the staff of Bellevue Baptist Church, Cordova, TN - a church of over 15,000 members. There he serves in the Pastoral Care/Benevolence Department. He is a member of the Mid-South Baptist Association Administrative Leadership Council, Mid-South Urban Coalition, IMPACT Fellowship (a fellowship of churches), and a member of one of the large interdenominational Christian athlete fellowships, FCA- Fellowship of Christian Athletes. Many, new and seasoned pastors alike regard him as a pastor of pastors.

He is the author of "Faith Developed in the Darkroom" and committed to sharing God's Word through practical messages that empower individuals to fulfill their destiny.

He has been married to Lenora C. Griffin for over 32 years, she labors with her husband and shares with him God's purpose, vision, and conquest in ministry. They are the proud parents of Davien Jaree, who walks alongside them in ministry.

This book is included in the Faith Developed in the Darkroom Series.

Additional copies of this book and *Faith Developed in the Darkroom* are available in your local bookstore or from:

Darryl O. Griffin

Darryl O. Griffin Ministries

P.O. Box 1333

Cordova, TN 38088

901.205.6991

www.darrylogriffin.com

www.ingramcontent.com/pod-product-compliance
Ingram Content Group UK Ltd.
Pitfield, Milton Keynes, MK11 3LW, UK
UKHW041822200726
13854UKWH00002BA/507

9 781734 658125